60 SILLY SONGS

A Collection of 60 Creative and Silly Songs
Arranged for Easy Piano with Lyrics, Chord Symbols
and Optional Very Easy Second Parts for Added Child Participation

Compiled, arranged and adapted by

ROGER EDISON

Author of

*A Family Album of
Favorite Nursery Songs*

GW00673030

Affectionately dedicated to children of all ages
who deserve to be silly at least once in a while,
and especially to
Anna, Jesi and Alexandra.

Roger Edison

Contents

Section 1 • Animals from Here and There Page Track

The Slitheree-Dee. 3 . . . 1

Boa Constrictor . . . . 4 . . . 2

The Lion. . . . . 6 . . . 3

The Monkey and the Elephant . . . . 8 . . . 4

The Clam . . . . 10 . . . 5

The Animal Fair. . . . . 12 . . . 6

Little Bunny Foo Foo. . . . . 14 . . . 7

One Grasshopper Jumped. . . . . 16 . . . 8

The Bear Went Over the Mountain . . . . 18 . . . 9

Ten Little Teddy Bears. . . . . 19 . . 10

Mary Had a William Goat . . . . 20 . . 11

Mules . . . . 21 . . 12

Section 2 • Kookie People and Crazy Places

Jack Sprat . . . . 22 . . 13

Betty Botter . . . . 23 . . 14

Michael Finnigin . . . . 24 . . 15

Father's Old Gray Whiskers. . . . . 25 . . 16

Three Jolly Fishermen . . . . 26 . . 17

Doctor Foster . . . . 27 . . 18

Peter Piper . . . . 28 . . 19

There Was a Crooked Man. . . . . 29 . . 20

Rub-A-Dub-Dub. . . . . 30 . . 21

John Jacob Jingleheimer Schmidt . . . . 31 . . 22

From Wibbleton to Wobbleton. . . . . 32 . . 23

Going to St. Ives. . . . . 33 . . 24

Section 3 • Camp Songs

Skidamarink . . . . 34 . . 25

I With I Were a Wittle Thugar Bun . . . . 36 . . 26

See-Saw, Sacra Down . . . . 38 . . 27

Ba, Be. . . . . 39 . . 28

Oh, You Can't Get to Heaven. . . . . 40 . . 29

The Green Grass Grows All Around . . . . . . 42 . . 30

There's a Hole in the Bucket
(Carla and Farley). . . . . 44 . . 31

It Ain't Gonna Rain . . . . 45 . . 32

The State Song . . . . 46 . . 33

If All the World Were Paper. . . . . 47 . . 34

Who Did?. . . . . 48 . . 35

Section 4 • Old-Time Silly Songs

The Centipede and the Frog. . . . . 49 . . 36

Shool . . . . 50 . . 37

Eating Goober Peas . . . . 52 . . 38

Two Little Flies . . . . 54 . . 39

Limericks . . . . 55 . . 40

Two Naughty Flies . . . . 56 . . 41

I Don't Want to Play in Your Yard. . . . . 58 . . 42

The Woodchuck Song . . . . 59 . . 43

Rig-Jag-Jig-Jag. . . . . 60 . . 44

Will You Walk a Little Faster? . . . . 62 . . 45

The King of the Cannibal Islands. . . . . 64 . . 46

Under the Bamboo Tree . . . . 66 . . 47

When Mosquitos Cackle . . . . 67 . . 48

The Three Flies. 68 . . 49

Section 5 • Parodies

Higgledy, Piggledy. . . . . 69 . . 50

John Brown's Baby . . . . 70 . . 51

We're Here Because. . . . . 71 . . 52

Be Kind to Your Web-Footed Friends . . . . . 72 . . 53

Tough Luck . . . . 73 . . 54

Starkle, Starkle, Little Twink . . . . 74 . . 55

The Peanut Song. . . . . 75 . . 56

Boola Boola . . . . 76 . . 57

Do Your Ears Hang Low? . . . . 77 . . 58

Mary's Coal Black Lamb . . . . 78 . . 59

Rip Your Pants . . . . 79 . . 60

Alphabetical Index 80

THE SLITHEREE-DEE

Words and Music by Shel Silverstein

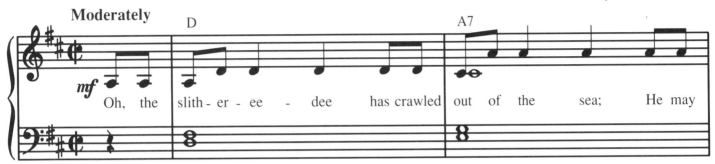

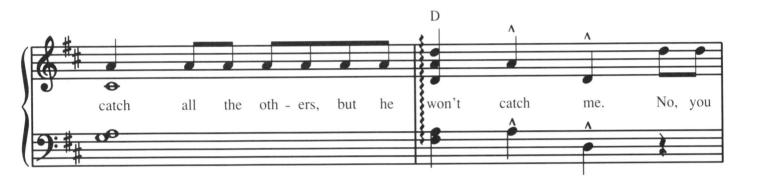

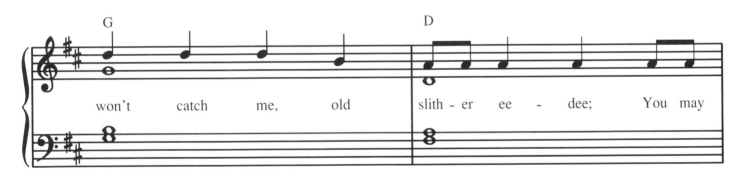

*Child's part

BOA CONSTRICTOR

Moderately

Words and Music by Shel Silverstein

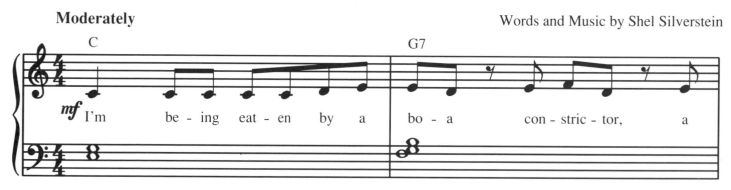

I'm being eat-en by a bo-a con-stric-tor, a

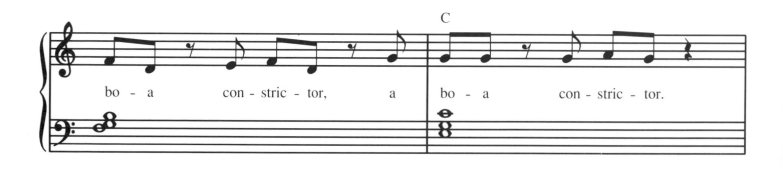

bo-a con-stric-tor, a bo-a con-stric-tor.

I'm being eat-en by a bo-a con-stric-tor, and I

don't like it one bit! Whad-da-ya know, it's nib-blin' my

toe. Oh, gee, it's up to my knee. Oh,

fid - dle, it's up to my mid-dle. Oh, heck, it's up to my

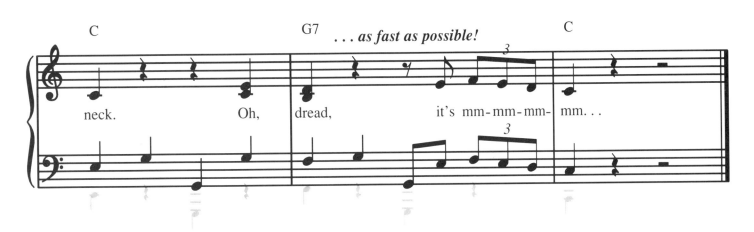

neck. Oh, dread, it's mm-mm-mm- mm...

* Child's part

THE LION

Moderately fast

Words and Music by Shel Silverstein

mf I am sing - ing this song from in - side of a li - on and it's

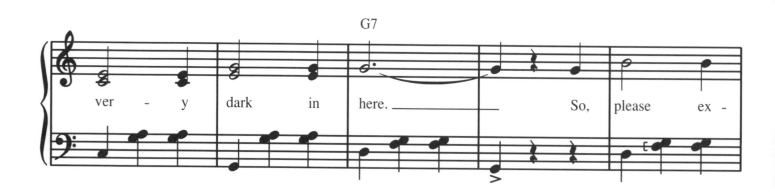

ver - y dark in here. _____ So, please ex -

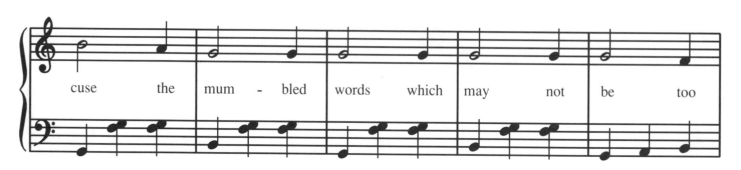

cuse the mum - bled words which may not be too

* Child's part

THE MONKEY AND THE ELEPHANT

Words and Music
by Shel Silverstein and Baxter Taylor

*Child's part

3. Now, the monkey said, "You're thinking like a donkey."
   A long time ago.
   "She's kinda small and you're sorta chunky."
   A long time ago.
   "So sit right down upon my knee;
   I'll tell you why your love can never be:
   It's a virtual impossibility."
   A long time ago.

4. Now, the elephant's tears went plink-e-ty plunky,
   A long time ago.
   And he went home to pack his trunkie,
   A long time ago.
   He said, "I see that bee was not for me."
   So he went and married a little gray flea,
   And they were as happy as they could be.
   A long time ago.

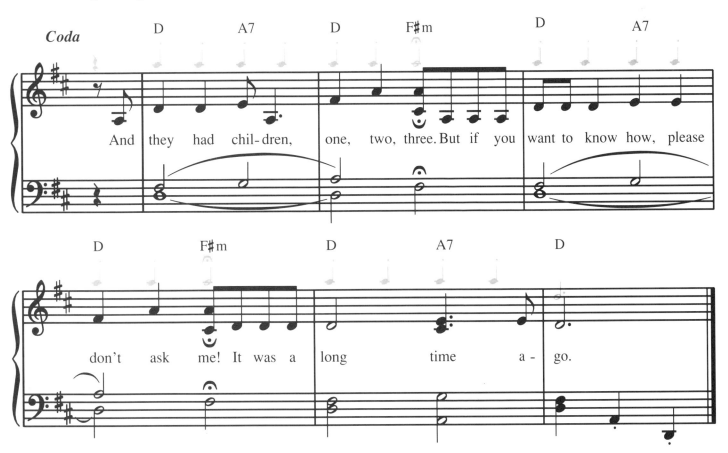

THE CLAM

Moderate waltz

Words and Music by Shel Silverstein

1. I found a clam be - side the sea in -
2. (I) put the clam clam in a pew - ter pot and I

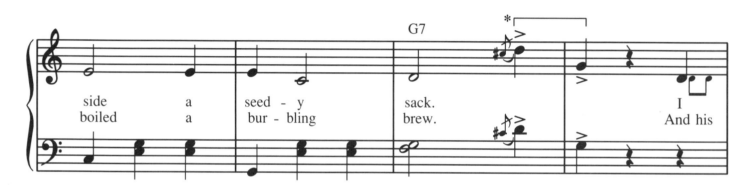

side a seed - y sack. I
boiled a bur - bling brew. And his

said to the clam, "Dear sir or ma'am, al -
green eyes__ gleamed and he steamed and steamed and he

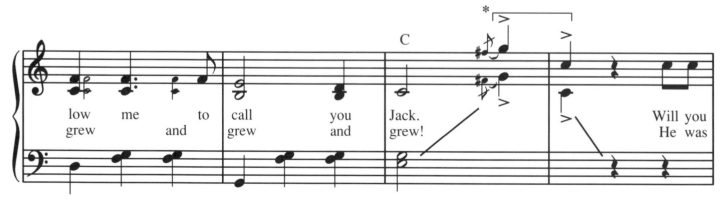

low me to call you Jack. Will you
grew and grew and grew! He was

*Upper notes (minus grace notes) can be used for child's part, one octave higher.

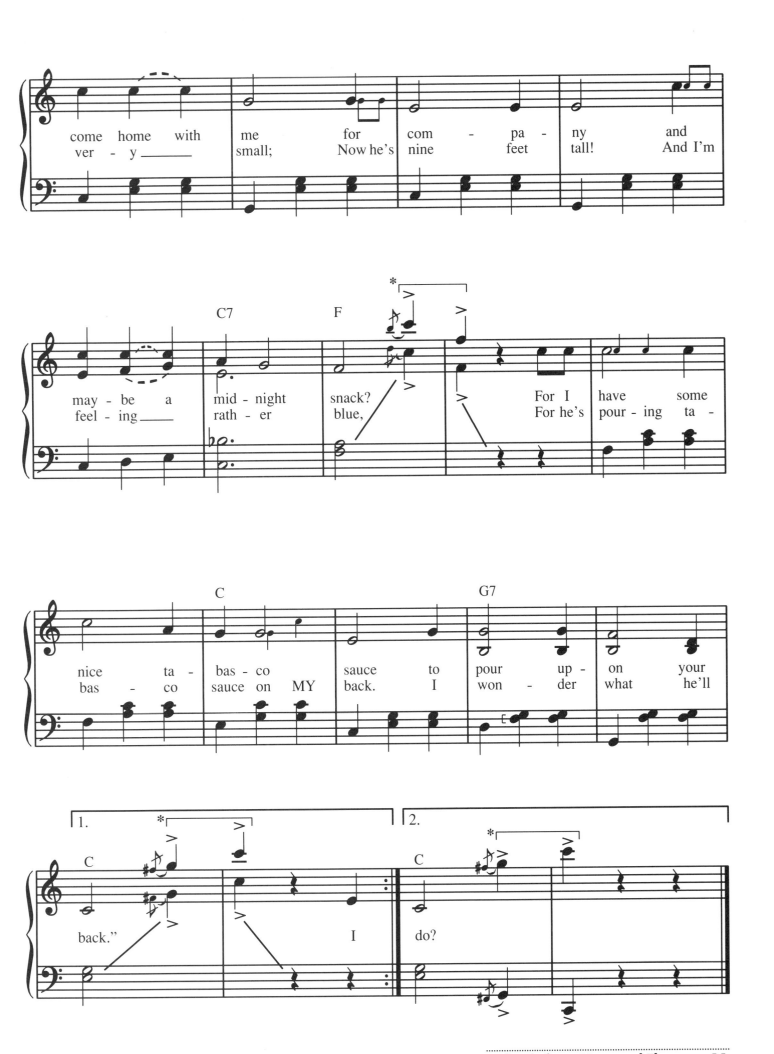

THE ANIMAL FAIR

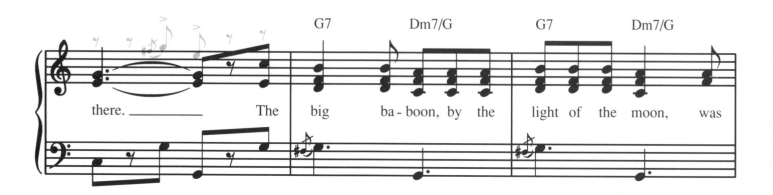

* Child's part

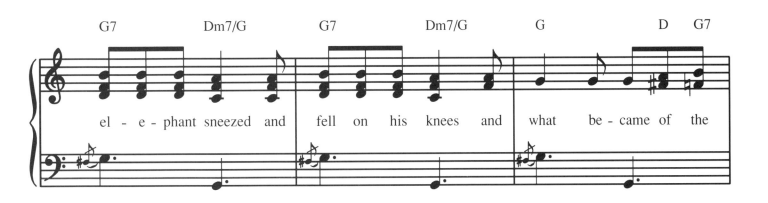

LITTLE BUNNY FOO FOO

Words: Traditional
Music: "Down by the Station"

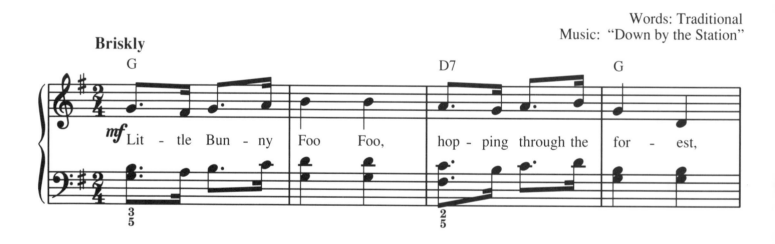

Lit - tle Bun - ny Foo Foo, hop - ping through the for - est,

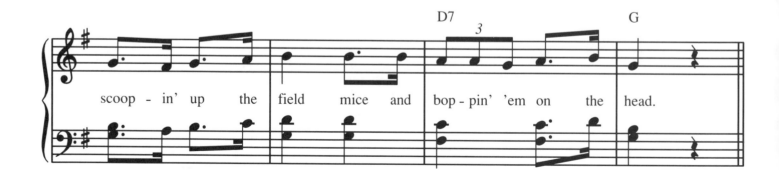

scoop - in' up the field mice and bop - pin' 'em on the head.

(Spoken): Then, down came the Good Fairy, and she said:

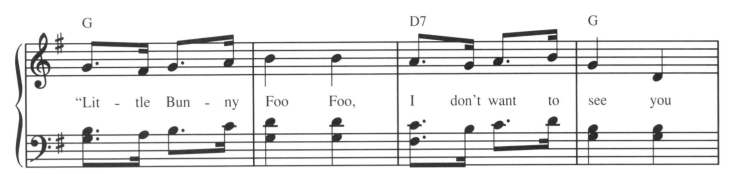

"Lit - tle Bun - ny Foo Foo, I don't want to see you

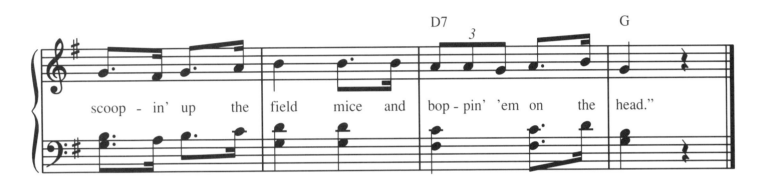

scoop - in' up the field mice and bop - pin' 'em on the head."

1. *(Spoken)* "I'll give you **three** chances, and if you don't behave, I'll turn you into a GORN!"
   Well, Little Bunny Foo Foo didn't know what a gorn was,
   but it didn't sound like anything he wanted to be turned into.
   Nevertheless, first thing the next morning:

   (Repeat from the beginning.)

2. "I'll give you **two** more chances, and if you don't behave I'll turn you into a GORN."

   (After a pause, repeat from the beginning.)

3. "I'll give you **one** more chance, and if you don't behave I'll turn you into a GORN."

   (After a pause, repeat from the beginning.)

4. "Little Bunny Foo Foo, I gave you three chances and you still didn't behave."

   And ***poof,*** she turned him into a GORN!

And the moral of this story is: Hare today, gorn tomorrow.

A child can mime the action:

"hopping through the forest"—make hopping motions with two fingers outstretched.
"scoopin' up the field mice"—make scooping motions with other hand.
"boppin' 'em on the head"—bop the imaginary mice.

ONE GRASSHOPPER JUMPED

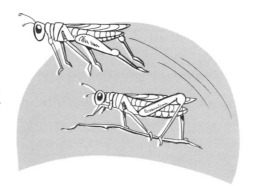

Words: Traditional
Music: "Battle Hymn of the Republic"

March tempo

One grass-hop – per jumped right o – ver the oth – er grass-hop – per's

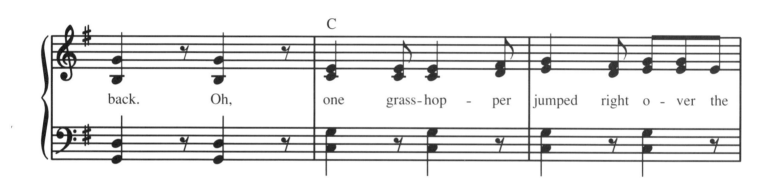

back.   Oh,   one grass-hop – per jumped right o – ver the

oth – er grass-hop – per's back.   One grass-hop – per

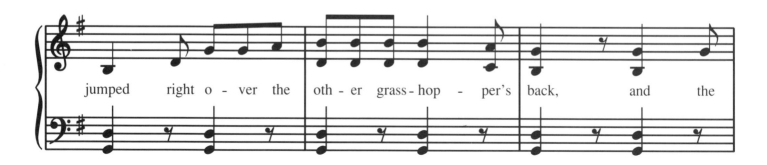

jumped right o – ver the oth – er grass-hop – per's back,   and the

*Child's part

THE BEAR WENT OVER THE MOUNTAIN

Words: Traditional
Music: "For He's a Jolly Good Fellow"

Like a slow march

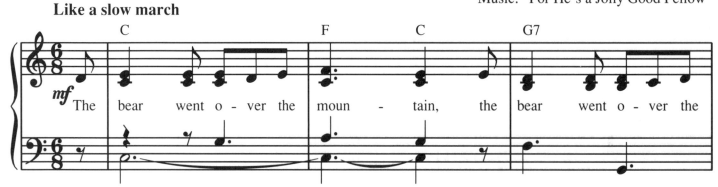

The bear went o-ver the moun - tain, the bear went o-ver the

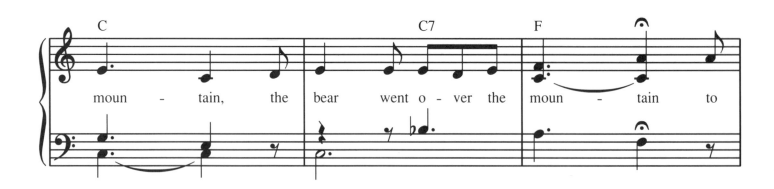

moun - tain, the bear went o-ver the moun - tain to

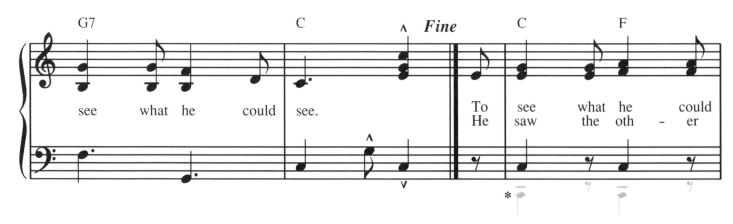

see what he could see. *Fine*

To see what he could
He saw what the oth - er

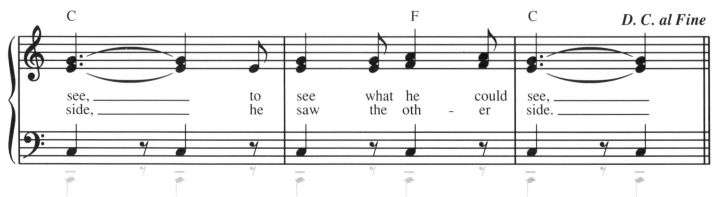

D. C. al Fine

see, _____ to see what he could see, _____
side, _____ he saw the oth - er side. _____

* Child's part

TEN LITTLE TEDDY BEARS

Words and Music by Roger Edison
Adapted from "99 Bottles"

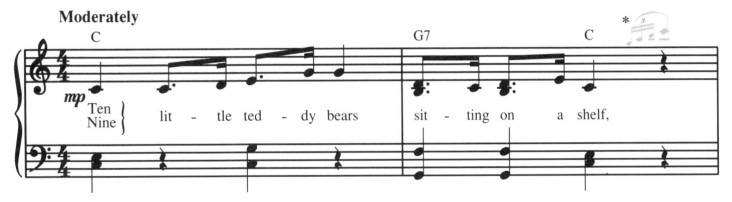

Continue similarly, until there are "no little teddy bears sitting on a shelf."

* Child's part is played 8va throughout.

MARY HAD A WILLIAM GOAT

Words: Traditional
Music: "Mary Had a Little Lamb"

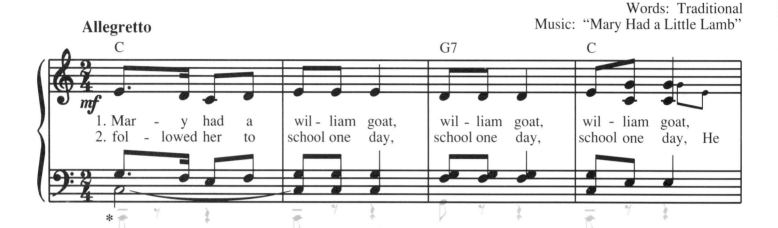

Allegretto

1. Mar - y had a wil - liam goat, wil - liam goat, wil - liam goat, school one day, school one day, school one day, He
2. fol - lowed her to

Mar - y had a wil - liam goat and he was lined with zinc. He
fol - lowed her to school one day and drank a pint of

ink. _____

* Child's part

3. Once he ate an oyster can, oyster can, oyster can,
   Once he ate an oyster can and a line of shirts.

4. The shirts can do no harm inside, harm inside, harm inside,
   The shirts can do no harm inside but, oh, that oyster can!

5. The can was filled with dynamite, dynamite, dynamite,
   The can was filled with dynamite which Billy thought was cheese.

6. He rubbed against poor Mary's shin, Mary's shin, Mary's shin,
   He rubbed against poor Mary's shin his deep distress to ease.

7. There was a flash of girl and goat, girl and goat, girl and goat,
   There was a flash of girl and goat and they were no more seen.

8. Mary's soul to heaven went, heaven went, heaven went,
   Mary's soul to heaven went and Billy's went to _____!

9. Whoop-de-doo-den-doo-den-day, doo-den-day, doo-den-day,
   Whoop-de-doo-den-doo-den-day, his went the other way.

MULES

Words: Traditional
Music: "Auld Lang Syne"

Firmly

On mules we find two legs be-hind, and two we find be-fore, We stand be-hind be-fore we find what the two be-hind be for. When we're be-hind the two be-hind we find what these be for, So stand be-fore the two be-hind, be-hind the two be-fore.

*Child's part: Child holds note for four measures each time.

JACK SPRAT

Traditional

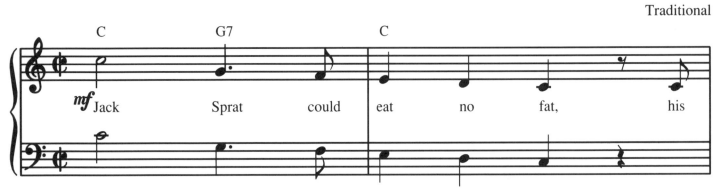

Jack Sprat could eat no fat, his wife could eat no lean. And so be - tween them

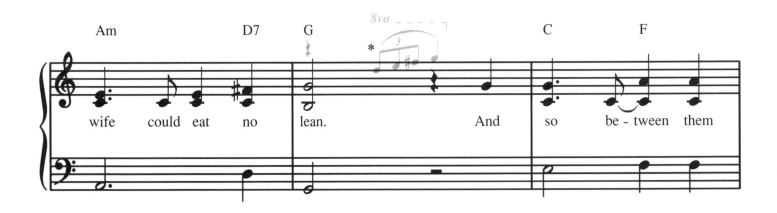

*

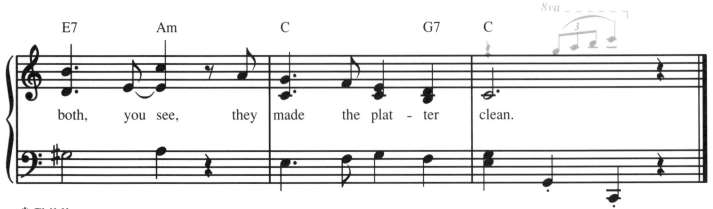

both, you see, they made the plat - ter clean.

*Child's part

BETTY BOTTER

Brightly

Words: Traditional
Music: "Yankee Doodle"

Child's part

MICHAEL FINNIGIN

Words: Traditional
Music: "Goin' to Boston"

Moderately

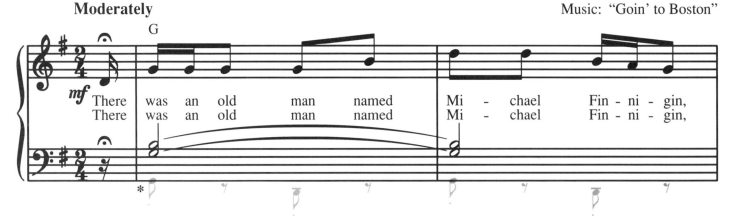

There was an old man named Mi - chael Fin - ni - gin,
There was an old man named Mi - chael Fin - ni - gin,

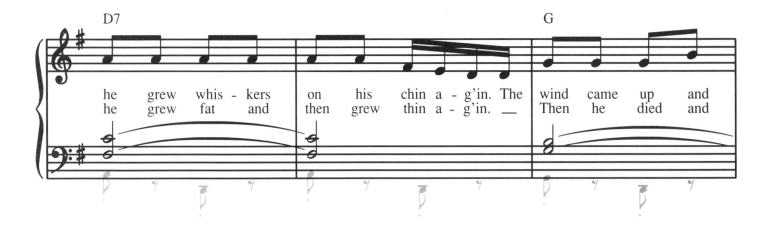

he grew whis - kers on his chin a - g'in. The wind came up and
he grew fat and then grew thin a - g'in. ___ Then he died and

blew them ___ in a - g'in; } Poor old Mi - chael Fin - ni - gin. Be - gin a - g'in:
had to be - gin a - g'in; }

* Child's part

**Keep repeating until the neighbors call the police!

FATHER'S OLD GRAY WHISKERS

*Child's part

THREE JOLLY FISHERMEN

Moderately

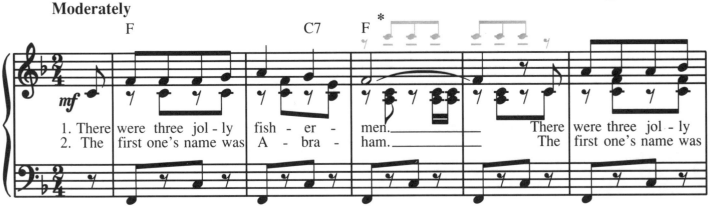

1. There were three jol-ly fish-er - men._____ There were three jol-ly
2. The first one's name was A - bra - ham._____ The first one's name was

fish-er - men._____ Fish-er, fish-er, men, men, men.
A - bra - ham._____ A - bra, A - bra, ham, ham, ham.

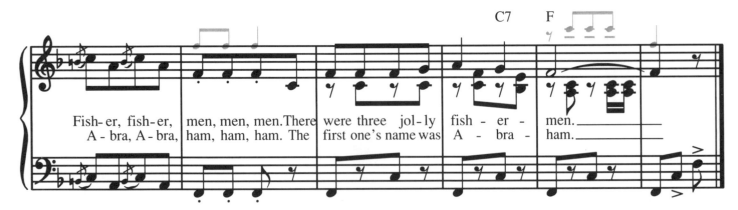

Fish- er, fish- er, men, men, men. There were three jol-ly fish-er - men._____
A - bra, A - bra, ham, ham, ham. The first one's name was A - bra - ham._____

* Child's part

3. The next one's name was Isaac.
The next one's name was Isaac.
Isa, Isa, zak, zak, zak.
Isa, Isa, zak, zak, zak.
The next one's name was Isaac.

4. The third one's name was Jacob.
The third one's name was Jacob.
Jaka, Jaka, cub, cub, cub.
Jaka, Jaka, cub, cub, cub.
The third one's name was Jacob.

5. They all sailed up to Amsterdam.
They all sailed up to Amsterdam.
Amster, Amster, shh, shh, shh.
Amster, Amster, shh, shh, shh.
They all sailed up to Amsterdam.

DOCTOR FOSTER

Words: Traditional
Music by Roger Edison

*Child's part

PETER PIPER

Words: Traditional
Music by Roder Edison

* Child's part

THERE WAS A CROOKED MAN

Traditional

Allegretto

mf

There was a crook-ed man and he walked a crook-ed mile. He found a crook-ed six - pence up - on a crook-ed stile. He bought a crook-ed cat which caught a crook - ed mouse, and they all lived to - geth - er in a crook - ed lit - tle house.

* Child's part

RUB-A-DUB-DUB

Allegretto

Traditional

Rub - a - dub - dub, three men in a tub, and who do you think they be? _____ The butch- er, the bak- er, the can- dle- stick mak- er, and all of them gone to sea. _____

* Child's part

JOHN JACOB JINGLEHEIMER SCHMIDT

Briskly

John Jacob Jingle-hei-mer Schmidt, his name is my name, too. When - ev - er we go out and peo-ple al-ways shout,

No chords

John Jacob Jin - gle - hei - mer Schmidt." Dah dah dah dah dah dah dah.

* Child's part

*Repeat as many times
as you want, and fade.*

FROM WIBBLETON TO WOBBLETON

Words: Traditional
Music by Roger Edison

With breathless haste

* Child's part

GOING TO ST. IVES

Words: Traditional
Music by Roger Edison

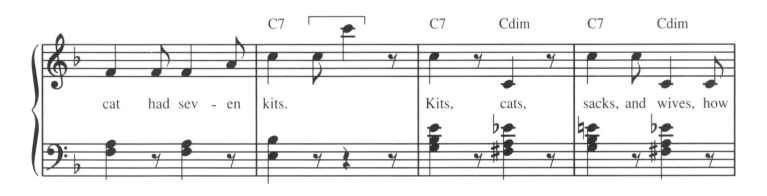

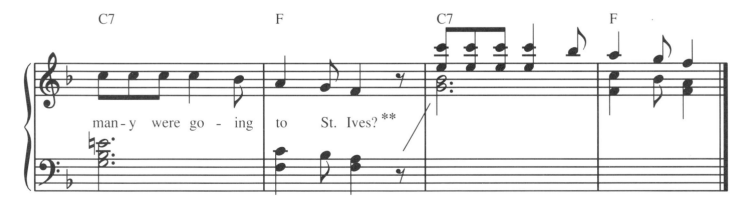

*Can be used as child's part.
**Answer: One

SKIDAMARINK

Soft-shoe tempo

Traditional

1. Skid - a - ma-rink - a rink - y dink - a skid - a - ma-rink - y doo,
**2. Skid - a - ma-wink - a wink - y dink - a skid - a - ma-wink - y doo,

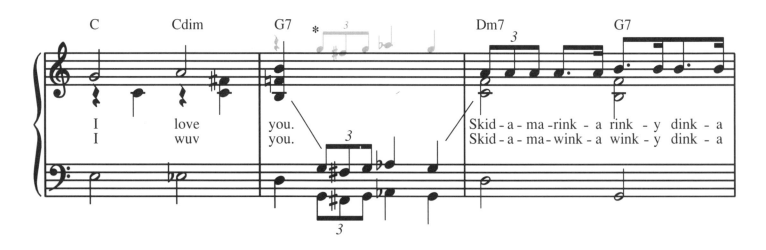

I love you.
I wuv you.

Skid - a - ma-rink - a rink - y dink - a
Skid - a - ma-wink - a wink - y dink - a

skid - a - ma-rink - y doo, I love you. I
skid - a - ma-wink - y doo, I wuv you. I

* Child's part
**Sing the second chorus in an Elmer Fudd voice.

*** Child may play top notes 1 octave higher.

I WITH I WERE A WITTLE THUGAR BUN

Traditional
New words by Roger Edison

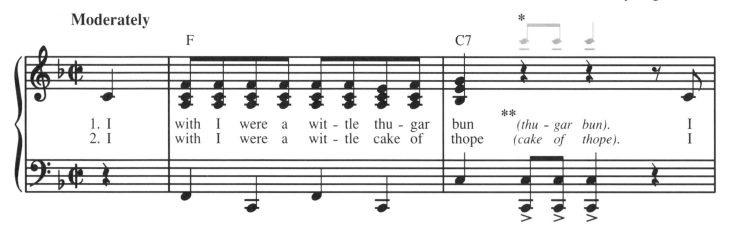

1. I with I were a wit-tle thu-gar bun *(thu-gar bun).* I
2. I with I were a wit-tle cake of thope *(cake of thope).* I

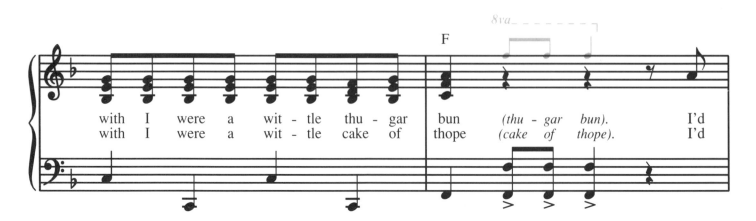

with I were a wit-tle thu-gar bun *(thu-gar bun).* I'd
with I were a wit-tle cake of thope *(cake of thope).* I'd

* Child's part
**Child sings echoes.

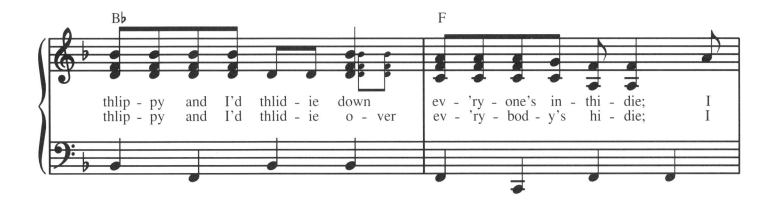

thlip - py   and   I'd   thlid - ie   down   ev - 'ry - one's   in   thi - die;   I
thlip - py   and   I'd   thlid - ie   o - ver   ev - 'ry - bod - y's   hi - die;   I

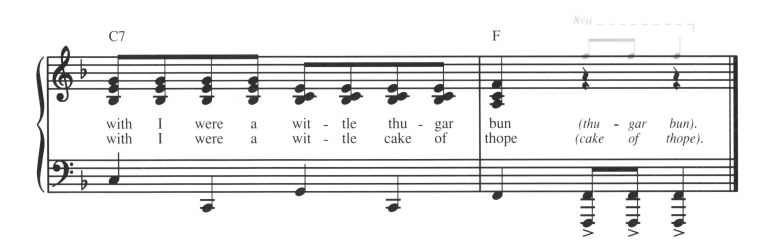

with   I   were   a   wit - tle   thu - gar   bun   *(thu - gar   bun).*
with   I   were   a   wit - tle   cake   of   thope   *(cake   of   thope).*

3. I with I were a monkey in the zoo (in the zoo). *(two times)*
    I'd thit upon the thelf and squatch my wittle thelf;
    I with I were a monkey in the zoo *(in the zoo).*

4. I with I were a wittle mothquito *(mothquito).* (two times)
    I'd buthie and I'd bitie under ev'rybody's nightie;
    I with I were a wittle mothquito *(mothquito).*

5. I with I were a fithie in the thea *(in the thea).* (two times)
    I'd thwim awound tho cute without a bathing thuit;
    I with I were a fithie in the thea *(in the thea).*

6. I with I were a wittle bog of mud *(bog of mud).* (two times)
    I would ooze and I would gooze inthide ev'rybody's thooze;
    I with I were a wittle bog of mud *(bog of mud).*

7. I with I were a wittle Englith thpawwow *(Englith thpawwow).* (two times)
    I'd thit up on a thteeple and I'd thpit on all the people;
    I with I were a wittle Englith thpawwow *(Englith thpawwow).*

8. I with I were a wittle kangawoo *(kangawoo).* (two times)
    I'd hippie and I'd hoppie inthide my mommie's pockie;
    I with I were a wittle kangawoo *(kangawoo).*

9. I with I were a wittle thtripie thkunk *(thtripie thkunk).* (two times)
    I'd thit up in the twees and perfume all the bweeze;
    I with I were a wittle thtripie thkunk *(thtripie thkunk).*

SEE-SAW, SACRA DOWN

Andante

Traditional

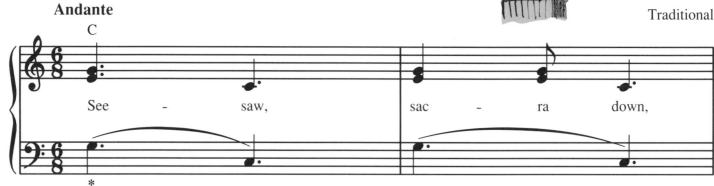

See - saw, sac - ra down,

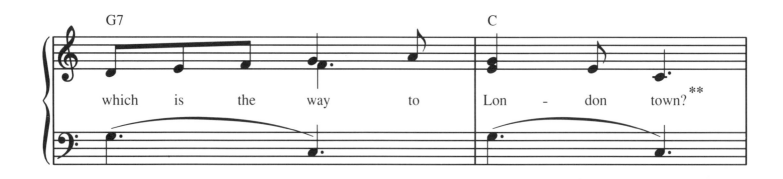

which is the way to Lon - don town?**

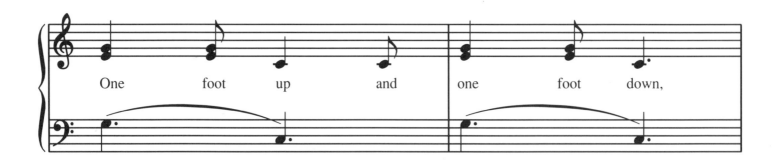

One foot up and one foot down,

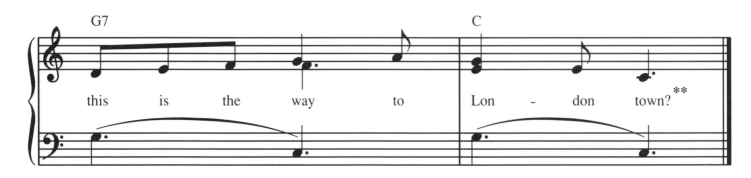

this is the way to Lon - don town?**

*Child's part doubles one octave lower.

**Or, substitute the name of your town here.

BA, BE

*Child's part

OH, YOU CAN'T GET TO HEAVEN

Traditional
New words by Roger Edison

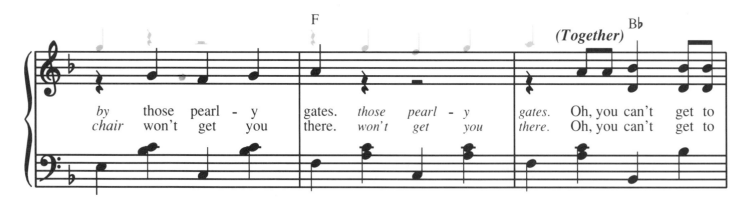

* Child's part
** Child sings echoes.

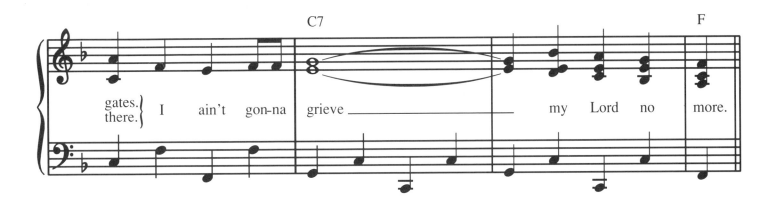

3. Oh, you can't get to heaven . . . in a brand new Porsche . . .
    'Cause a brand new Porsche . . . costs too much, of corsche . . .
    (repeat together)

4. Oh, you can't get to heaven . . . in a four by four . . .
    'Cause a four by four . . . won't fit through the door . . .
    (repeat together)

5. Oh, you can't get to heaven . . . in a Thunderbird . . .
    In a Thunderbird? . . . That's just absurd! . . .
    (repeat together)

6. But if you get there . . . before I do . . .
    Just dig a hole . . . and pull me through . . .
    (repeat together)

THE GREEN GRASS GROWS ALL AROUND

Traditional

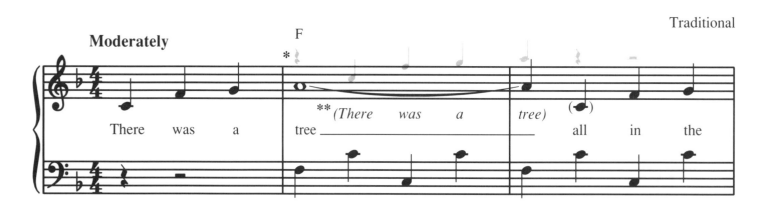

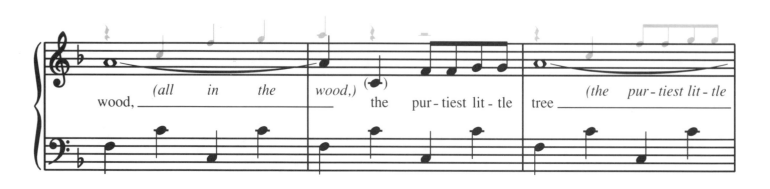

*Child's part
**Child sings echoes.

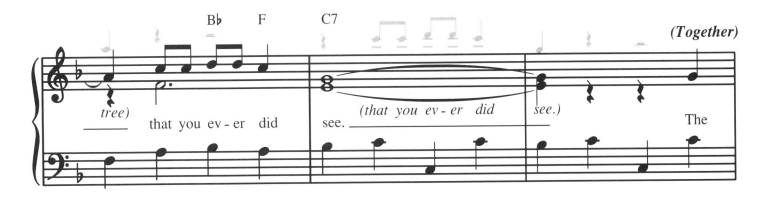

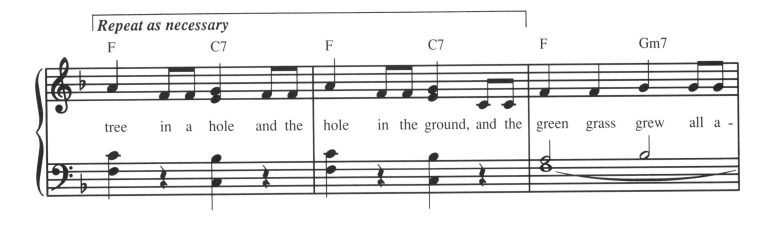

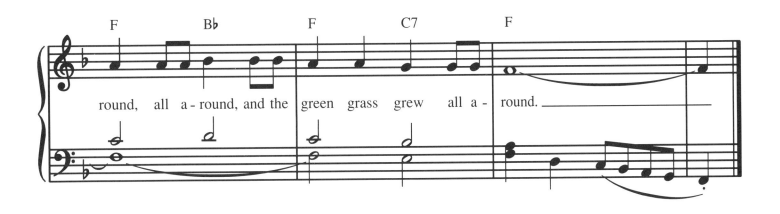

2. And on that tree . . . there was a limb . . .
   The purtiest little limb . . . that you ever did see . . .
   The limb on the tree
   And the tree in a hole,
   And the green grass grew all around, all around,
   And the green grass grew all around.

3. And on that limb . . . there was a branch . . .
4. And on that branch . . . there was a nest . . .
5. And in that nest . . . there was an egg . . .
6. And in that egg . . . there was a bird . . .
7. And on that bird . . . there was a wing . . .
8. And on that wing . . . there was a feather . . .
9. And on that feather . . . there was a bug . . .
10. And on that bug . . . there was a germ . . .

THERE'S A HOLE IN THE BUCKET
(CARLA AND FARLEY)

Traditional
New words by Roger Edison

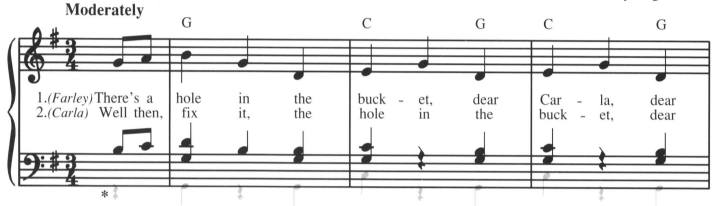

1. *(Farley)* There's a hole in the buck - et, dear Car - la, dear
2. *(Carla)* Well then, fix it, the hole in the buck - et, dear

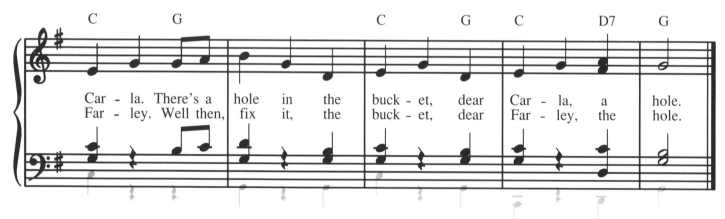

Car - la. There's a hole in the buck - et, dear Car - la, a hole.
Far - ley. Well then, fix it, the buck - et, dear Far - ley, the hole.

* Child's part

3. With what shall I fix it? . . .
4. With a straw you shall fix it . . .
5. But the straw is too long . . .
6. Then cut it . . .
7. With what shall I cut it? . . .
8. With a knife . . .
9. But the knife is too dull . . .
10. Then whet it . . .
11. With what shall I whet it? . . .

12. With a whetstone . . .
13. But the whetstone's too dry . . .
14. Then wet it . . .
15. But with what shall I wet it? . . .
16. With water, with water . . .
17. But how shall I carry it? . . .
18. In a bucket, a bucket . . .
19. But there's a hole in the bucket . . .

(start again from the beginning)

IT AIN'T GONNA RAIN

Traditional
New words by Roger Edison

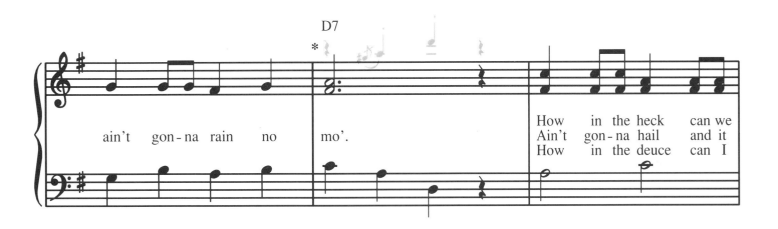

* Child's part

THE STATE SONG

Words adapted by Roger Edison
Music: "It Ain't Gonna Rain"

Briskly

mf

1. Oh, what did Ten - nes - see, boys, oh,
2. Oh, what did Ten - nes - see, boys, oh,

what did Ten - nes - see? Oh, what did Ten - nes -
what did Ten - nes - see? A - las - ka - gain as a

see, ___ boys, oh, what did Ten - nes - see?
per - son - al friend ___ what did Ten - nes - see?

*Child's part

3. She saw what Arkansas, girls,
   I tell you again.
   Oh, where has Oregon, girls?
   She's taking Oklahome.

4. Oh, how did Wisconsin, boys?
   She stole a Newbrasskey.
   Oh, what did Connecti-cut, boys?
   She cut Mississip-pi.

5. Oh, what did Delaware, girls?
   She wore a New Jersey.
   Oh, where did Ida-hoe, girls?
   She hoed her Maryland.

6. Oh, what did Io-way, boys?
   She weighed a Washing-ton.
   How did Flora-die, boys?
   She died in Missouri (misery).

7. What did little Georgia do?
   She drank a Mini-soda.
   This song's about the different states
   And that's the Maine idea.

IF ALL THE WORLD WERE PAPER

Skipping along

Traditional

mf If all the world were pa - per and

all the sea were ink, and if all the trees were

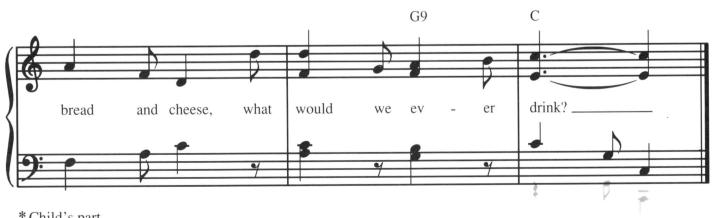

bread and cheese, what would we ev - er drink? ___

*Child's part

WHO DID?

Briskly

Traditional

1. Who did, who did, who did, who did, who did swal - low Jo, Jo, Jo, Jo?
2. Whale did, whale did, whale did, whale did, whale did swal - low Jo, Jo, Jo, Jo.

Who did, who did, who did, who did, who did swal - low Jo, Jo, Jo, Jo?
Whale did, whale did, whale did, whale did, whale did swal - low Jo, Jo, Jo, Jo.

Who did, who did, who did, who did, who did swal - low Jo, Jo, Jo, Jo?
Whale did, whale did, whale did, whale did, whale did swal - low Jo, Jo, Jo, Jo.

Who did, swal - low Jo - nah, swal - low Jo - nah down?
Whale did, swal - low Jo - nah, swal - low Jo - nah down.

*Child's part

3. Dan'l, Dan'l, Dan'l, Dan'l, Dan'l in the li, li, li, li. *(three times)*
   Dan'l in the lion, in the lion's den.

4. Gabriel, Gabriel, Gabriel, Gabriel, Gabriel blow your trum, trum, trum, trum. *(three times)*
   Gabriel blow your trumpet, blow your trumpet loud.

THE CENTIPEDE AND THE FROG

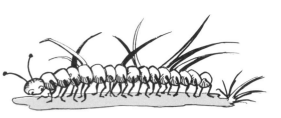

Words and Music by Walter Jones

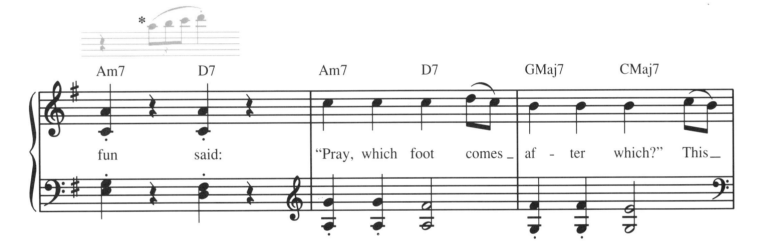

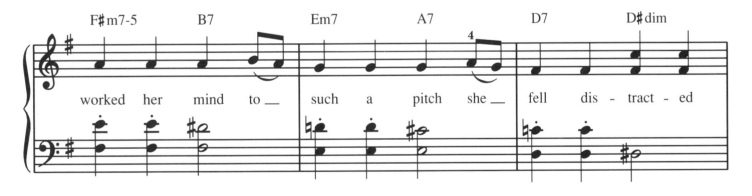

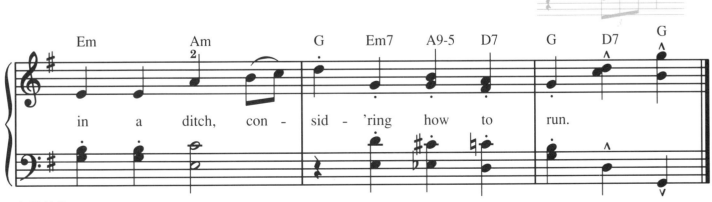

*Child's part

SHOOL

Lively

Traditional

1. I wish I was in Bos - ton cit - y where
2. (I) wish I was on yon - der hill ___ for

all the girls they are so pret - ty. If I did - n't have a time 'twould
there I'd sit and cry so my fill ___ and ___ ev - 'ry ___ drop could

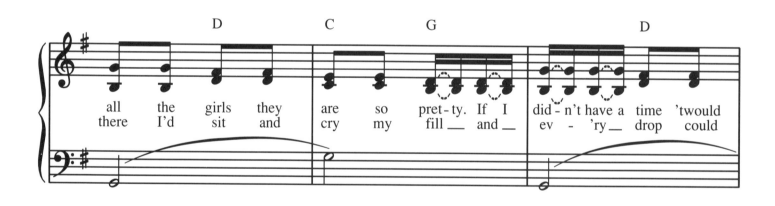

be a pit - y,
turn a mill, ___ } dis - cum bib - ble lol - la - boo, slow reel.

* 8va

* Child's part

Chorus

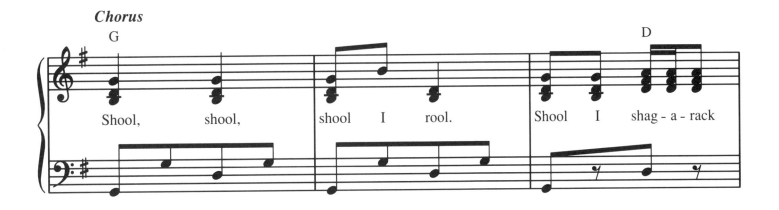

Shool, shool, shool I rool. Shool I shag-a-rack

shoo-la bar-ba-cool. The first time I saw psil-ly bal-ly eel, dis-cum

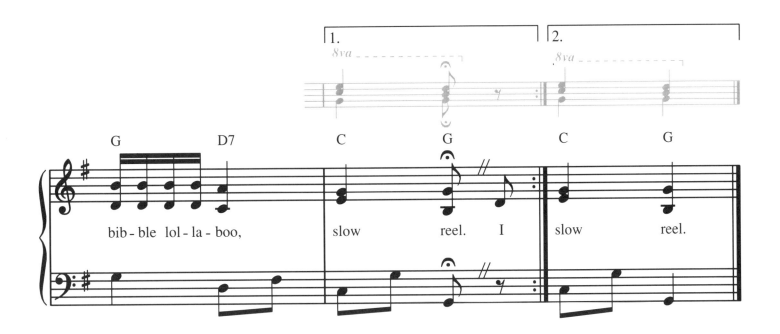

bib-ble lol-la-boo, slow reel. I slow reel.

Traditional

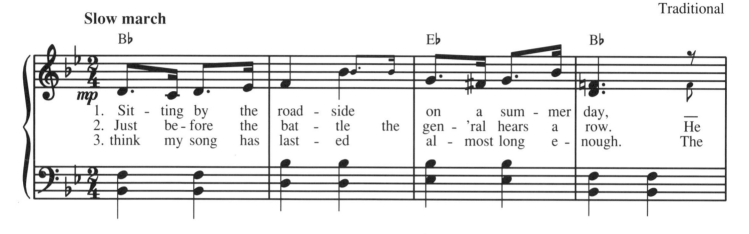

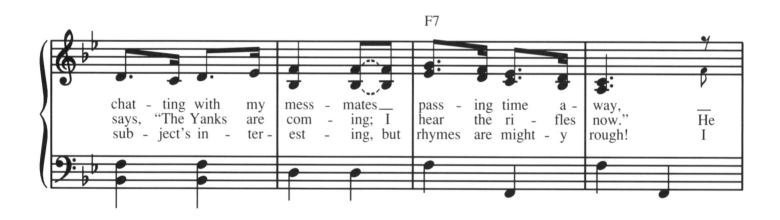

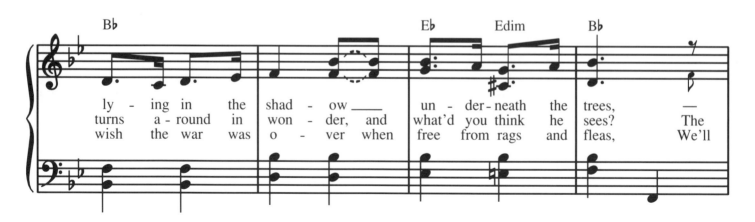

*Goober peas are peanuts.

Goodness how delicious!___ **Eating goober peas.**
Tennessee militia___ **eating goober peas.**
kiss our wives and sweethearts and gobble goober peas.

Peas, peas, peas, peas, eating goober peas.

Goodness how delicious, eating goober peas.

eating goober peas.

peas.

**Child's part

TWO LITTLE FLIES

Words and Music by W. B. Olds
Adapted by Roger Edison

Moderately

Two lit-tle flies, two lit-tle flies, two lit-tle flies, two lit-tle flies,

two lit-tle flies, two lit-tle flies. There were two lit-tle flies in a

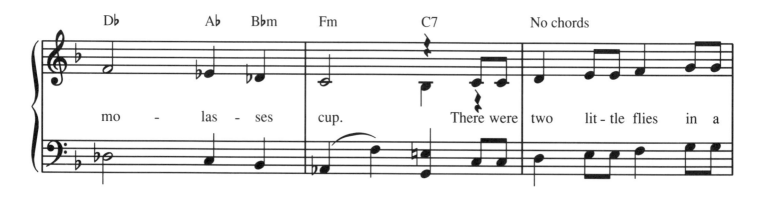

mo - las - ses cup. There were two lit-tle flies in a

mo-las-ses cup, but they would-n't speak to me, they were so stuck-up!

*Child's part

LIMERICKS

Words and Music by Alfred Williams
New words by Roger Edison

Allegretto

1. There was an old la - dy from Woos - ter _____ who was
2. A can - ner, ex - ceed - ing - ly can - ny, _____ on one
3. A nan - ny, whose first name was Fan - ny, _____ on one

ver - y an - noyed by a roos - ter. _____ So she cut off his head un -
morn - ing re - marked to his gran - ny, _____ "Oh, a can - ner can can an - y -
morn - ing re - marked to her gran - ny, _____ "Oh, a gran - ny in France can _

til he was dead, and _ now he don't crow like he use - ter. _____
thing that he can, but a can - ner can't can a can, can he?" _____
dance in her pants, but a gran - ny can't can - can, or can she?" _____

*Child's part

TWO NAUGHTY FLIES

Words by Howard Willis
Music by Dan Braman
New words by Roger Edison

Allegretto

1. There were two flies, the sto - ry goes, and ___
2. (So) off they flew and did not stop till they

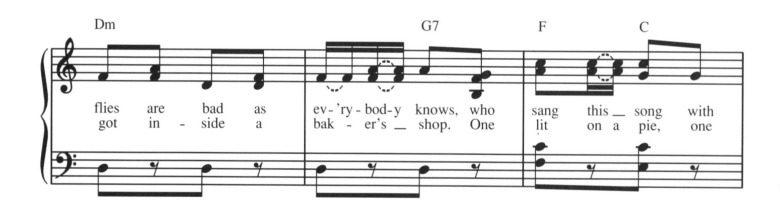

flies are bad as ev - 'ry - bod - y knows, who sang this ___ song with
got in - side a bak - er's ___ shop. One lit on a pie, one

buzz ___ and ___ hum: "Let's ___ go ___ have a time for the sum - mer's come."
in the muf - fin pan, 'cause they did - n't give a darn for the bak - er man.

Chorus:

*Child's part (optional)

3.   The blue fly hid in a doughnut hole,
      Then danced a jig on a hot French roll.
      The black fly sat on a cinnamon bun
      And licked off the sugar crumbs one by one.
(Chorus)

4.   And when they'd sampled ev'rything
      They started off upon the wing
      Buzzing a song with this refrain:
      "Goodbye, sweetheart, till I see you again."
(Chorus)

5.   Now, if you're inclined to be a little fly
      Just get a pair of wings and eat some cake and pie.
      But don't overdo it and take care where you light
      Or you'll land in the soup when you think you're all right!
(Chorus)

I DON'T WANT TO PLAY IN YOUR YARD

Words by Philip Wingate
Music by H. W. Petrie
New words by Roger Edison

*Child's part

THE WOODCHUCK SONG

Words by Bob Davis
Music by Ted Morse

*Child's part

RIG-JAG-JIG-JAG

Words and Music by Alfred Williams
New words by Roger Edison

Moderately

1. There was a girl named Di - nah o - ver there, o - ver there. There
2. I wish I was a geese___ o - ver there, o - ver there. I
3. I wish I was a cow___ o - ver there, o - ver there. I

was a girl named Di - nah o - ver there, o - ver there. There
wish I was a geese___ o - ver there, o - ver there. I
wish I was a cow___ o - ver there, o - ver there. I

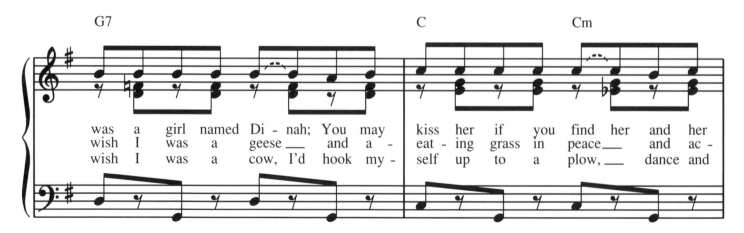

was a girl named Di - nah; You may kiss her if you find her and her
wish I was a geese___ and a - eat - ing grass in peace___ and ac -
wish I was a cow, I'd hook my - self up to a plow, ___ dance and

* Child's part

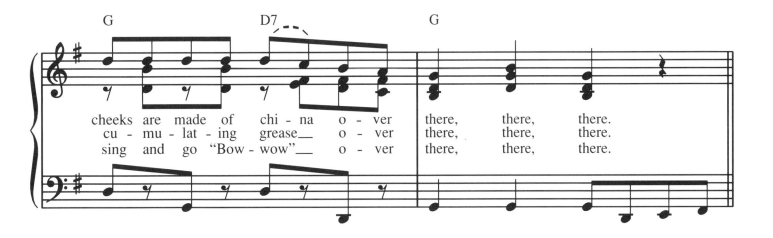

cheeks are made of chi - na o - ver there, there, there.
cu - mu - lat - ing grease___ o - ver there, there, there.
sing and go "Bow - wow"___ o - ver there, there, there.

Chorus:

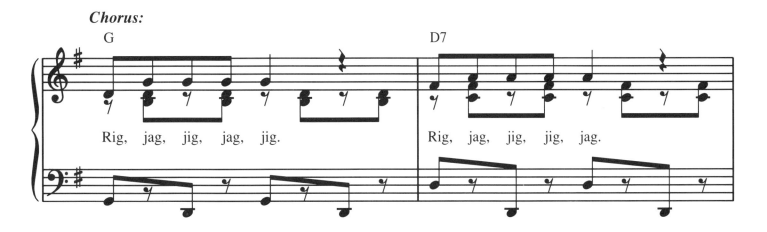

Rig, jag, jig, jag, jig.   Rig, jag, jig, jig, jag.

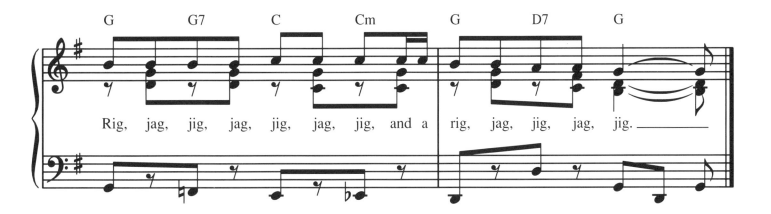

Rig, jag, jig, jag, jig, jag, jig, and a   rig, jag, jig, jag, jig. ___

4. I wish I was a monkey over there, over there.
   I wish I was a monkey over there, over there.
   I wish I was a monkey, dye my hair all green and punky,
   Then I'd be a funky monkey over there, there, there. *(Chorus)*

5. I wish I was a pig over there, over there.
   I wish I was a pig over there, over there.
   I wish I was a pig, eat a fig and dance a jig,
   Be a figgie, jiggy, piggie over there, there, there. *(Chorus)*

WILL YOU WALK A LITTLE FASTER?

Words and Music by A. S. Gratty

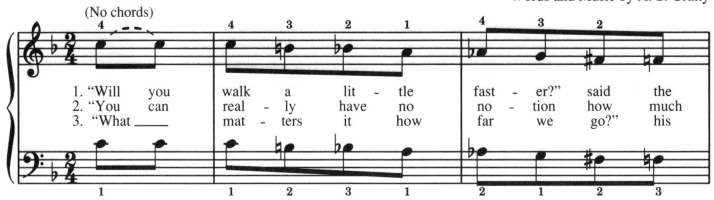

1. "Will you walk a lit - tle fast - er?" said the
2. "You can real - ly have no no - tion how much
3. "What ____ mat - ters it how far we go?" his

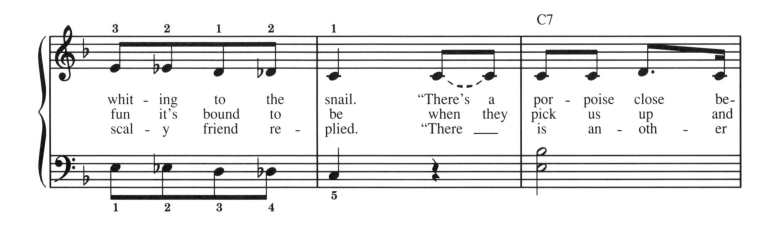

whit - ing to the snail. "There's a por - poise close be-
fun it's bound to be when they pick us up and
scal - y friend re - plied. "There ____ is an - oth - er

hind me and he's tread - ing on my tail. See how
throw us with the lob - sters out to sea." But the
shore, you know, up - on the oth - er side. The ____

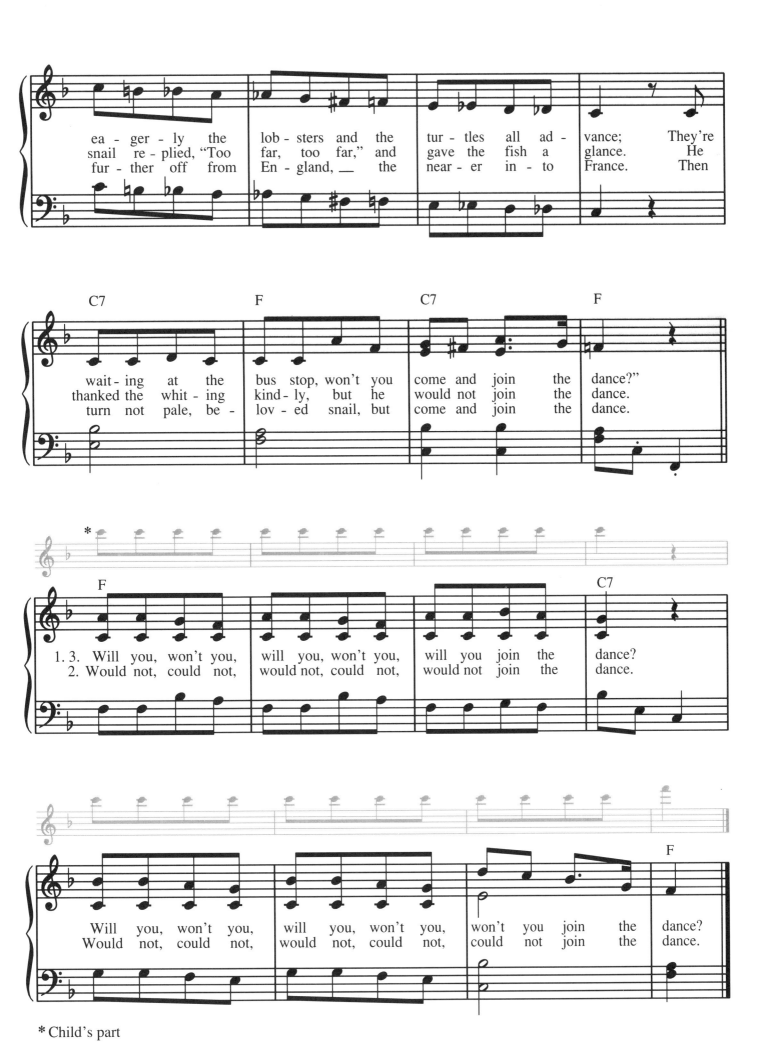

*Child's part

THE KING OF THE CANNIBAL ISLANDS

Moderately

Traditional

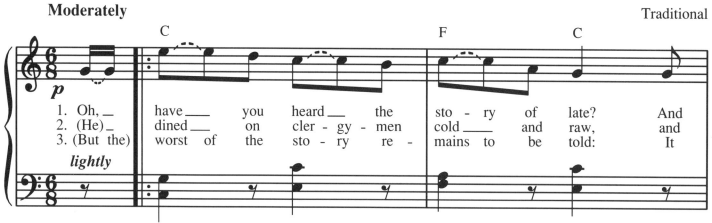

1. Oh, __ have __ you heard __ the sto - ry of late? And
2. (He) __ dined __ on cler - gy - men cold __ and raw, And and
3. (But the) worst of the sto - ry re - mains to be told: It

lightly

if __ you've not __ it's all in my pate, a - bout __ a might - y
slaugh - tered them all with - out li - cense or law. He nev - er took less at a
did not a - gree with his earth - ly mold. He died __ of eat - ing

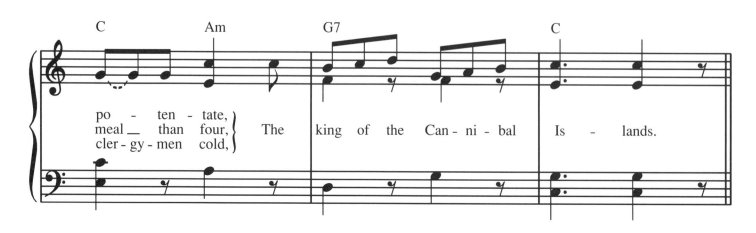

po - ten - tate,
meal __ than four, } The king of the Can - ni - bal Is - lands.
cler - gy - men cold,

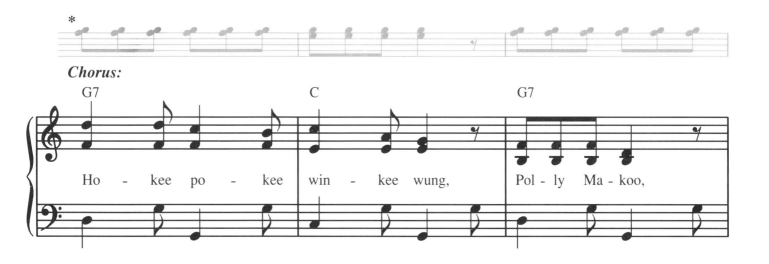

Chorus:

G7   **C**   **G7**

Ho - kee po - kee win - kee wung,   Pol - ly Ma - koo,

C   **F**   **C**   **Am**

Ko - mo - ling Kung.   Han - ga - ree, wan - ga - ree, chin - chi - ring chung,   The

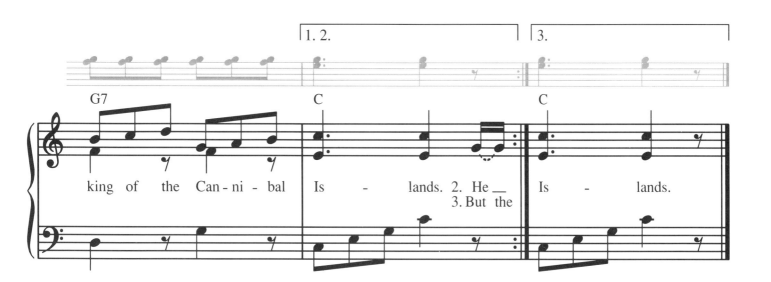

1. 2.   3.

G7   **C**   **C**

king of the Can - ni - bal Is - lands. 2. He __ Is - lands.

3. But the

*Child's part is played an octave higher than written throughout.

UNDER THE BAMBOO TREE

Words and Music by Bob Cole

*Child's part

WHEN MOSQUITOS CACKLE

Words and Music by Ned Sletwa
Adapted by Roger Edison

*Child's part

THE THREE FLIES

Words by Alfred Williams
Music: Traditional

Moderately

1. There were three flies, once up- on a time, de-
2. The first was a yel-low one, the sec-ond was blue. The

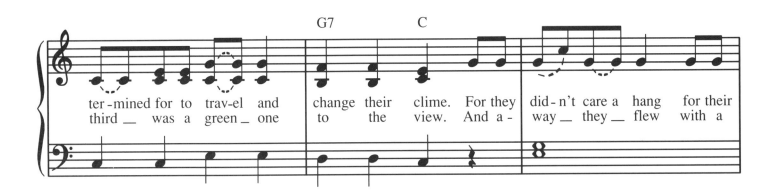

ter-mined for to trav-el and change their clime. For they did-n't care a hang for their
third was a green one to the view. And a- way they flew with a

fa- ther, nor their moth- er, nor their un- cle, nor their aunt, nor their
"hi ho hum," sing- ing as they went, "Glo- ry

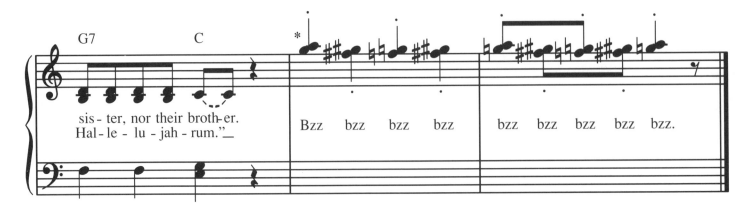

sis- ter, nor their broth- er. Bzz bzz bzz bzz bzz bzz bzz bzz bzz.
Hal- le- lu- jah- rum."

* Can be used as child's part.

HIGGLEDY, PIGGLEDY

Words: Traditional
Music: "Hickory, Dickory, Dock"

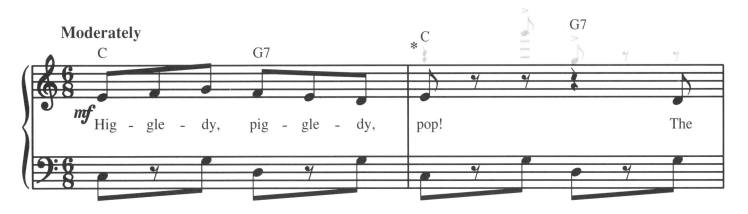

Higgledy, piggledy, pop! The

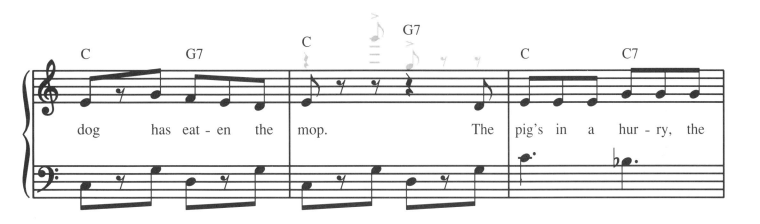

dog has eaten the mop. The pig's in a hurry, the

cat's in a flurry. Higgledy, piggledy, pop!

*Child's part

JOHN BROWN'S BABY

Words: Traditional
Music: "Battle Hymn of the Republic"

March tempo

John Brown's ba - by had a cold up-on its chest,

John Brown's ba - by had a cold up-on its chest, John Brown's ba - by had a

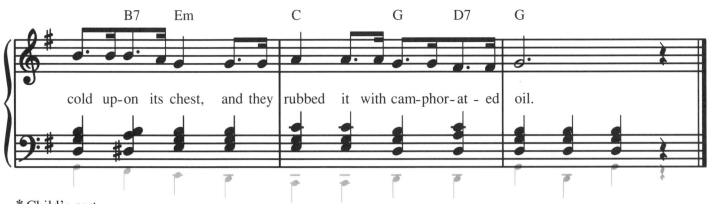

cold up-on its chest, and they rubbed it with cam-phor-at - ed oil.

*Child's part

This song is sung six times.

1. Sing as written.
2. Substitute a rocking motion for the word "baby."
3. Substitute a rocking motion for baby and a sneeze for the word "cold."
4. Substitute as in number 3 and also slap chest for the word "chest."
5. Substitute as in number 4 and also rub chest for the word "rubbed."
6. Substitute as above and also substitute holding nose and making a funny face for the words "camphorated oil."

WE'RE HERE BECAUSE

Words: Traditional
Music: "Auld Lang Syne"

Moderately

We're here be-cause we're here be-cause we're here be-cause we're

here, we're here be-cause we're here be-cause we're here be-cause we're

here. We're here be-cause we're here be-cause we're here be-cause we're

here, we're here be-cause we're here be-cause we're here be-cause we're here.

*Child's part

BE KIND TO YOUR WEB-FOOTED FRIENDS

Words: Traditional
Music: "Stars and Stripes Forever"

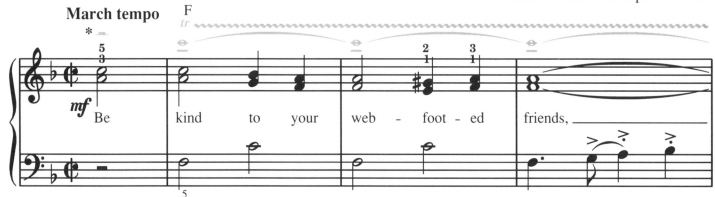

Be kind to your web - foot - ed friends, ____

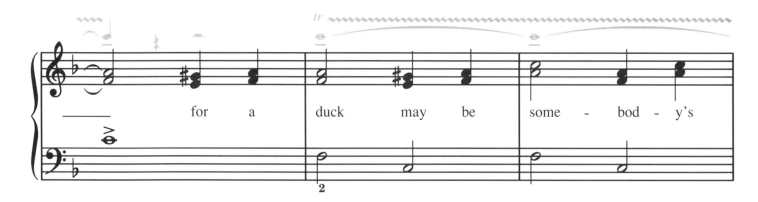

____ for a duck may be some - bod - y's

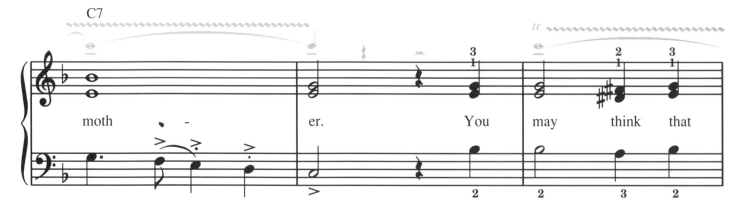

moth - er. You may think that

this is the end, ____ and it is!

*Child's part is played 8va higher throughout.

TOUGH LUCK

Words adapted by Roger Edison
Music: "Turkey in the Straw"

Briskly

mf

1. Oh, his horse went dead and his mule went lame, and he lost six cows, what a mea-sly shame! Then a hur-ri-cane came on a sum-mer's day and blew the house where he lived a-way. An hole in the ground!

2. (An earth-quake came when his house was gone, and it swal-lowed up the land that the house stood on. Then the tax col-lec-tor came a-round and charged him up with the

1. **2.**

* Child's part

STARKLE, STARKLE, LITTLE TWINK

Words: Traditional
Music: "Twinkle Twinkle, Little Star"

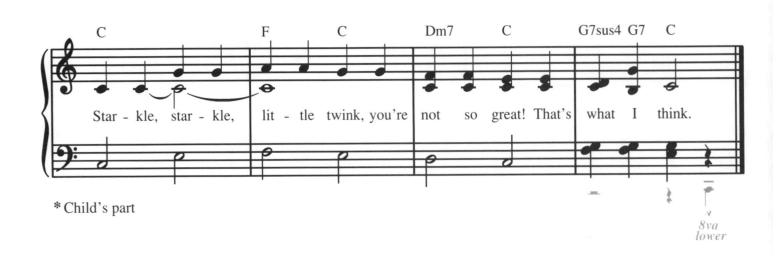

*Child's part

THE PEANUT SONG

Words: Traditional
Music: "Polly Wolly Doodle"

Moderately

A — pea - nut sat on a rail - road track, his

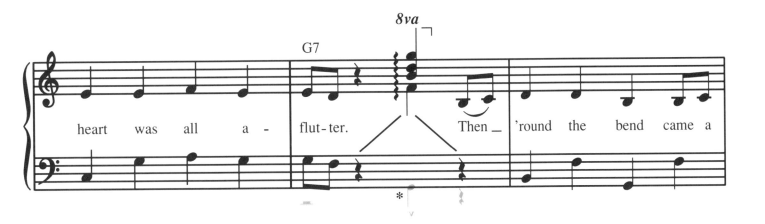

heart was all a - flut-ter. Then — 'round the bend came a

rail - road train: Toot! Toot! Pea - nut but - ter! Squish!

*Child's part

BOOLA BOOLA

Words and Music by Goodwin and Hirsch
New words by Roger Edison

March tempo

Boo - la boo - la, _____ boo - la boo - la, _____

_____ boo - la boo - la, _____ boo - la boo - la.

Give me one more _____ _____ coo - ka coo - la, _____
Let me see you _____ dance the hu - la, _____
Teach - er hit me _____ with a roo - la, _____

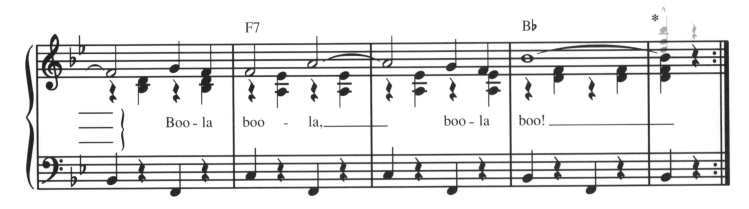

Boo - la boo - la, _____ boo - la boo! _____

*Child's part

Continue similarly with:
Take a visit to the zoo-la . . .
Take a dive in-to the pool-a . . .

DO YOUR EARS HANG LOW?

Words: Traditional
Music: "Turkey in the Straw"

Do your ears hang low? Do they wob-ble to and fro? Can you tie 'em in a knot? Can you tie 'em in a bow? Can you throw 'em o'er your shoul-der like a

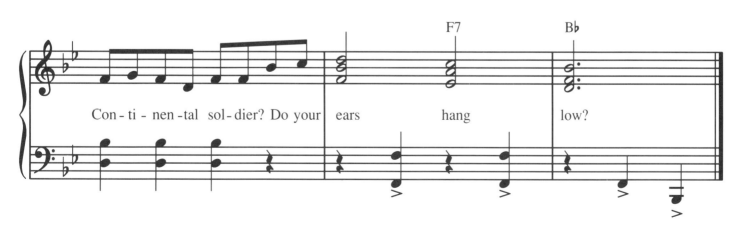

Con-ti-nen-tal sol-dier? Do your ears hang low?

MARY'S COAL BLACK LAMB

Moderately

Words by Ken Foy
Music: "Mary Had a Little Lamb"

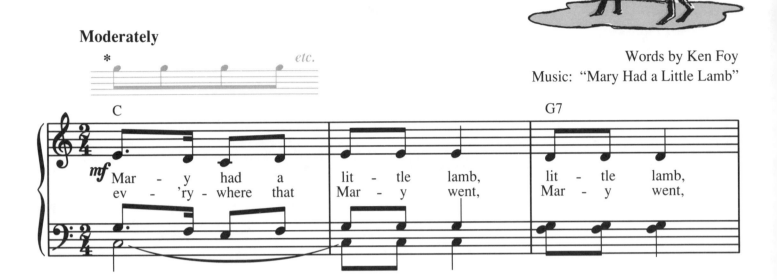

Mar - y had a lit - tle lamb, lit - tle lamb,
ev - 'ry - where that Mar - y went, Mar - y went,

lit - tle lamb. Mar - y had a lit - tle lamb, its
Mar - y went, Ev - 'ry - where that Mar - y went, the

1.
fleece was black as coal. 'Cause

2.
lamb kept fall - ing in a big mud hole!

*Child's part

RIP YOUR PANTS

Words: Traditional
Music: "Row, Row, Row Your Boat"

Briskly

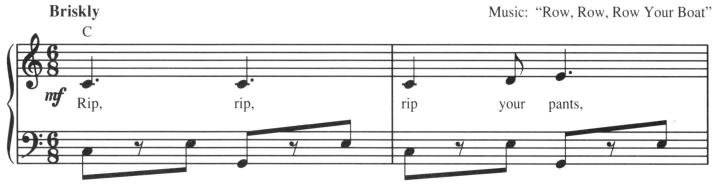

Rip, rip, rip your pants,

rip paper *

gent - ly down the seam, *sfz* Mer - ri - ly, mer - ri - ly,

scream! *

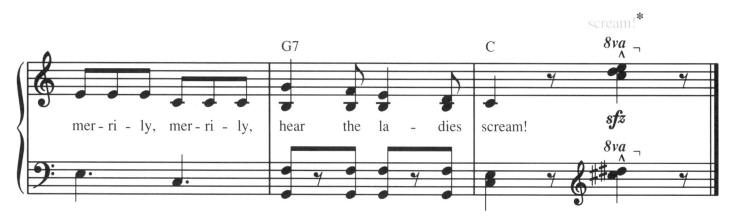

mer - ri - ly, mer - ri - ly, hear the la - dies scream!

* Child's part

Alphabetical Index

Animal Fair, The 12

Ba, Be 39

Bear Went Over the Mountain, The 18

Be Kind to Your Web-Footed Friends............72

Betty Botter 23

Boa Constrictor 4

Boola Boola.....................................76

Centipede and the Frog, The 49

Clam, The 10

Doctor Foster....................................27

Do Your Ears Hang Low? 77

Eating Goober Peas 52

Father's Old Gray Whiskers........................25

From Wibbleton to Wobbleton.....................32

Going to St. Ives.................................33

Green Grass Grows All Around, The............42

Higgledy, Piggledy 69

I Don't Want to Play in Your Yard 58

If All the World Were Paper 47

It Ain't Gonna Rain 45

I With I Were a Wittle Thugar Bun 36

Jack Sprat 22

John Brown's Baby 70

John Jacob Jingleheimer Schmidt 31

King of the Cannibal Islands, The.................64

Limericks...55

Lion, The 6

Little Bunny Foo Foo 14

Mary Had a William Goat.............................20

Mary's Coal Black Lamb 78

Michael Finnigin 24

Monkey and the Elephant, The 8

Mules...21

Oh, You Can't Get to Heaven.....................40

One Grasshopper Jumped.............................16

Peanut Song, The.................................75

Peter Piper 28

Rig-Jag-Jig-Jag...................................60

Rip Your Pants...................................79

Rub-A-Dub-Dub....................................30

See-Saw, Sacra Down 38

Shool 50

Skidamarink 34

Slitheree-Dee, The...............................3

Starkle, Starkle, Little Twink 74

State Song, The 46

Ten Little Teddy Bears 19

There's a Hole in the Bucket
(Carla and Farley)...............................44

There Was a Crooked Man.........................29

Three Flies, The.................................68

Three Jolly Fishermen 26

Tough Luck 73

Two Little Flies 54

Two Naughty Flies 56

Under the Bamboo Tree 66

We're Here Because 71

When Mosquitos Cackle 67

Who Did? 48

Will You Walk a Little Faster? 62

Woodchuck Song, The 59